TREASURE HUNTER'S HANDBOOK

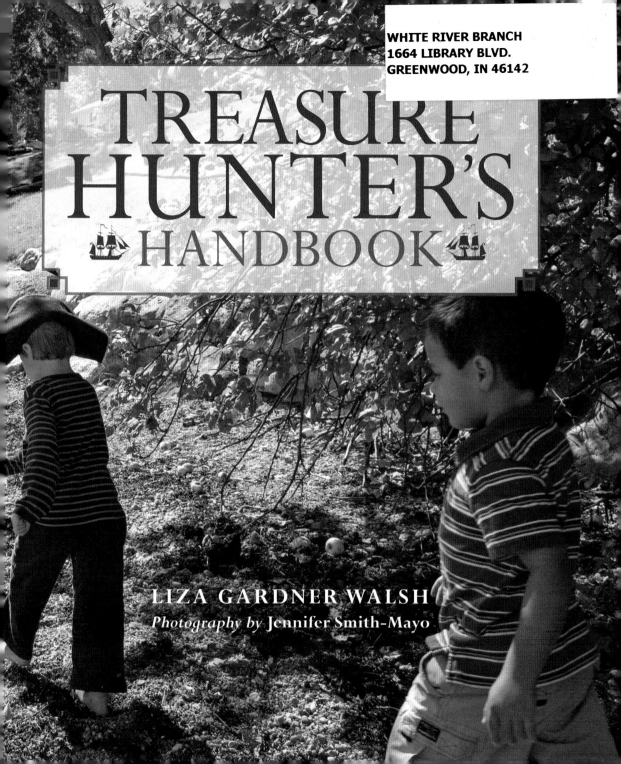

TREASURE HUNTER'S HANDBOOK

LIZA GARDNER WALSH

Photography by Jennifer Smith-Mayo

Published by Down East Books
A wholly owned subsidary of The Rowman & Littlefield Publishing Group, Inc.
4501 Forbes Boulevard, Suite 200, Lanham, MD 20706
www.rowman.com

16 Carlisle Street, London W1D 3BT, United Kingdom

Distributed by NATIONAL BOOK NETWORK

Copyright © 2014 by Liza Gardner Walsh
Photographs © 2014 by Jennifer Smith-Mayo
Designed by Lynda Chilton, Chilton Creative

British Library Cataloguing in Publication Information Available

Library of Congress Cataloging-in-Publication Data Available

ISBN 978-1-60893-278-8 (cloth : alk. paper)
ISBN 978-1-60893-279-5 (electronic)

♾™ The paper used in this publication meets the minimum requirements of American
National Standard for Information Sciences—Permanence of Paper for Printed Library
Materials, ANSI/NISO Z39.48-1992.

To my father, Philip Gardner,
for making every family outing into
an adventure.

Table *of* Contents

Introduction
The Quest Begins

Do you remember your very first treasure hunt? The thrill of finding that clue and all the others leading you to the jackpot? How about the first time you found a shard of pottery or a piece of quartz crystal? Or a coin that was more than a few years old? There is a thrill in hunting for treasure that few things in life can match. Who can resist the steady beep of a metal detector when it has sensed a find, the glimmer of gold in a river, or the challenge of finding a well-hidden geocache on a mountainside. Treasure hunting is as much about the hunt as the treasure. It is about potential and hope. You never know what's in store for you when you start on a treasure hunt. Maybe you will be like the man in Australia who found a 61-pound chunk of gold with a metal detector that then sold for a million dollars! But sometimes, many times, you won't find a thing, whether it's a failed geocache hunt or a metal-detecting mission that only turns up rusty old nails. The beauty of this hobby is that there is always tomorrow, there is always the next hunt, the chance that the next beep on your metal

detector will be something amazing.

Come with me as we explore a variety of treasure-hunting activities. We will cover the ins and outs of geocaching, letterboxing, metal detecting, hunting for rocks and minerals, and panning for gold, as well as the lure of buried treasure. We will also talk about how sometimes the best treasures of all are the things you kick up on your walk around the block—a smooth stone that fits right in the palm of your hand, or a perfect four-leaf clover. Maybe it is the piece of volcanic rock that gives you the final proof that your house is sitting on an ancient volcano. Many of these activities have creeds, which are general guidelines to follow that will make the activity safe and more enjoyable for you and will not harm the world around us. Here are a few of my own to add to the general creed of treasure hunting: Be curious, get outside, appreciate nature, explore, bring your family and friends and spend quality time together, and, most importantly, have fun.

Here's the thing: treasure hunting is about looking deeply at what you normally take for granted. It's about solving a problem. If you treasure hunt for long enough, maybe even for the rest of your life, you will

develop some really important skills. You will know the world around you better. You will develop patience, curiosity, and wonder. And, most likely, you will have a dresser top filled with things that tell stories from your hunts. You will pick up each one and remember the day you found it, where you were, and who you were with. It is these stories that are the real treasure. For, as renowned treasure hunter C.J. Stevens says, "Whatever you find here and keep will become a piece of your life. By lifting this from the earth, you carry it into the future." So onward, treasure hunter, the quest is waiting, and remember the joy that is in the hunt. As Bill Garrett said, "What I do is really not the pursuit of happiness but the happiness of pursuit." ☠

X Marks the Spot
Pirates and Buried Treasure

Many of you are probably well versed in pirate lore. For example, you might be aware that Blackbeard lit his beard on fire and had fourteen wives. When you close your eyes and think about those scallywags, you probably picture men with wooden legs, eye patches, hooks for hands, and parrots on their shoulders. There are tons of cool facts about these wolves of the sea, but this is a book about treasure. And throughout history, who happened to acquire lots of treasure? That's right, pirates. These sea-roving men, and sometimes women, were masters at acquiring fortunes and once they had all that loot, they either spent it quickly or buried it.

The daily life of pirates was not all that interesting. Bad food, bad pay, dangerous work, poor living conditions, and poor health. So can you blame them when they finally seized a ship or two and had the chance to brighten things up a little and dream of treasure coming their way? Well, we can blame them for being violent thieves, but let's get

back to the treasure and the question as to why they buried it in the first place.

The answer has to do with the origin of pirates. Piracy began in the 1500s, when owners of small British ships were given permission to capture the cargo from ships flying enemy flags. In return, these privateers, as they were known, could keep a small portion of the pirated goods and then give the rest of the booty to the king or queen. Many of the ships targeted by these privateers were Spanish galleons heading home from South and Central America, their holds filled with gold, silver, and exotic jewels. But this loose and supposedly equitable privateering soon got out of balance. One captain might tattle to the king about a ship whose privateers took too much loot for themselves, and then that ship became hunted by the Royal Navy. As it fled, the royal flag was taken down and replaced by a renegade pirate flag, and a band of pirates was born. Now this ship, laden with treasures, might be on the lookout for a good hiding spot to bury the spoils.

So began the practice of burying treasure. Many pirates buried their treasure between voyages to avoid being overtaken by a Royal ship or another pirate ship. Some pirates were known to have different caches hidden up and down the East Coast. The most renowned pirates are famous as much for their legendary lost buried treasure as their intense pirating. For example, Black Sam Bellamy's ship, the *Whydah,* carrying

$100,000 in gold and silver, sank somewhere off the coast of Cape Cod. Buried under the sea, this treasure was discovered by a man named Barry Clifford, who searched for many years before discovering this trove. Clifford created a museum called the Whydah Pirate Museum in Provincetown, Massachusetts, to display all the amazing artifacts found on Black Sam's ship. There is also supposedly an old fortification in Down East Maine where Black Sam buried what some say are 180 fifty-pound bags of gold deep in an underground chamber. This treasure has yet to be found, but people have found $1.5 million worth of treasure on Deer Isle in Maine, purported to belong to good old Black Sam himself.

Captain Kidd is known to have buried his treasures on a dozen or more islands up and down the coast, and estimates of the value are said to be in the millions. Blackbeard was known to be a master at hiding treasure in Maine. It is also rumored that he buried some treasure in a "certain wood on a certain ledge" near the town line between Brooklyn Connecticut, and Hampton, Connecticut. Even though evidence exists and many people have searched, this particular cache has never been found. On the night before his death, when asked where his treasure was buried, Blackbeard told his crew, "Nobody but myself and the Devil knows where it is, and the longest liver shall take all." Are you the one who will take all?

According to treasure hunter C.J. Stevens, "It is because of the dangerous nature of their calling—there was always the risk of being wrecked at sea or boarded and slaughtered by another crew—that the pirates never retrieved some of these treasures. Riches are still there waiting for us." This is where you come in. Many people have indeed found buried pirate treasure. One story from 1840 tells of a farmer named Samuel Grindle who was

hauling wood with his son when he discovered a coin. By the time the sun set, he had found twenty more, all from different countries. The quest was delayed by a big snowfall and the coming of winter, but that spring, father and son found more than

four hundred coins that were definitely of pirate origin.

HOW CAN YOU FIND BURIED TREASURE

Not all buried treasures are from pirates. Throughout history, banks have failed and people pulled their savings out, preferring to bury them in their backyards, especially during the 1930s with the Great Depression. Some people just plain distrust banks and prefer to have their fortunes sealed in a tin can and buried under a favorite tree. There is a story of a man who was cutting down an old elm tree in his yard when his chain saw began to spark and out spilled a fountain of silver coins. Someone had hidden their treasure not under a tree, but inside it! This means there is a lot more treasure to be found than just the loot from pirate ships. But the big question remains, how do you find this treasure?

Metal detecting is a good way to start, and lucky for you there is an entire chapter about it in this book! But finding this long-buried treasure will require you to become a pirate detective. Learn everything you can about these rogues. Many old books, especially the ones written by Edward Rowe Snow such as *The True Tales of Pirates and Their Gold,* give details on shipwrecks and the history of piracy. Go to pirate festivals and talk to the people who reenact the lives of pirates, as they spend much time researching the lives and myths of pirates. Fishermen and schooner captains know the ins and outs of the coastline and the hidden spots on islands. They also have been known to spin a yarn or two and might have heard some tales of intrigue concerning buried treasure. Maybe you're lucky enough to have a boat in your family or know someone who does, and you can research some trips to islands that are rumored to have treasure on them, such as any of the forty or more islands near Harpswell, Maine, that are said to be dotted with hidden caches. Not all pirates buried their treasure by the coast or on islands, as we are often

led to believe from books like *Treasure Island* by Robert Louis Stevenson, despite the fact that four islands in the state
of Maine alone are called Treasure Island. Author Patricia
Hughes writes of other buried-treasure sites in her book,
Lost Loot: Ghostly New England Treasure Tales. She tells of
treasure hidden in the Longfellow Mountains of western
Maine, the White Mountains of New Hampshire, and the
Green Mountains of Vermont. She even tells of one of the
most feared pirates of all, Edward Low, who is said to
have buried treasure on the road from Maine to Canada.

  If you want to get your hands on this treasure, you
are going to have to step in line behind some of the people who have
spent their entire lives searching. But you are young, curious, and
clever, and with a little luck and a lot of research, you just may find that
magical X that marks the spot. ☠

Pieces of Eight

Most pirate treasure chests are filled with what are known as pieces of eight.

These coins were made in Peru, Colombia, Mexico, and various other South American countries for almost three hundred years.

They are pure gold and silver and flattened into an irregular round shape with a picture of the Spanish coat of arms on one side and the cross of the Catholic Church on the other side.

Many people refer to these coins as doubloons.

In Colonial days, pieces of eight were chosen to be the standard currency and stayed in use until the Civil War.

One of these coins today is worth several hundred dollars, with rare versions fetching close to a thousand dollars.

Making a Treasure Map

Take a piece of regular paper and put it in a baking pan filled with your parents' leftover black coffee. Soak it overnight.

Let it dry and then rub a wet tea bag over the front.

Have a grownup burn the edges over a sink. This is best if the paper is still a little damp so the paper won't burn too quickly. Use a pencil to draw some sort of a treasure route. Imagine being on an island and draw certain landmarks near the buried treasure site. Draw an X where the treasure is and then draw a dotted line to mark the path to find it.

Old maps often have a compass rose and mythical beasts to signify the unknown with the quote "Here there be monsters." Get creative and have fun.

When you are finished, you can roll your map up and tie it with a ribbon. Perhaps you want to store this treasure map in an old bottle, but make sure to have it at the ready for any kind of impromptu treasure hunt that may arise.

{23}

Gold Fever
Panning for Gold

"Playfulness is a prospector's greatest strength when trying to unlock the mysteries on the next bend of the river."

— C.J. Stevens

 an you really catch a fever from gold? Or get a bite from a gold bug? Well, spend one day on a gold-producing river, with a pan in your hand, and I guarantee you will know what these sayings mean. Calling up images of the Wild West, the gold rush, and pioneers, gold hunting is alive and well today and is a great activity for the entire family. Take a gently rushing river, a sunny summer day, and a bunch of kids on a quest for gold, and you have the ingredients for a day that you won't forget and one that may even make you rich!

Just as any kind of treasure hunt demands patience, gold panning is no exception. Many start a day of panning thinking they are going to find chunks of gold to rival Indiana Jones. But any future gold hunter best set their mind to working because it takes a lot of digging around to find a real nugget and not just "fool's gold" (pyrite) or mica. Panning takes practice and grit. So, channel your inner '49er (which is what people from the California gold rush were called) pay attention to the following tips on panning, and you will have a head start on your quest for riches.

As you start on this path, you are now called a prospector. A prospector is anyone who explores an area for mineral deposits. A "prospect" is something that might happen in the future, and in the case of panning for gold, it means you might actually find what is known as "the mother lode!"

FINDING A PLACE IN THE RIVER

The first step in your hunt is to find a gold-producing river. Gold is a mineral that is found in sediment. Sediment is the crushed-up remains of rocks that were dragged by glaciers millions of years ago. Or when the bedrock, which is the solid rock that makes up the earth's crust, eroded. Over time, bits of gold have been pulled out of the bedrock and can now be found in the sandy bottoms of rivers. How do you know if the river that runs

near your house is filled with gold? Gold can be found in nature throughout all of the fifty states, but not always in quantities that make it worth prospecting. The good news is that about half of the states have enough gold to dig for. The best source to determine if you have gold nearby is your state government's website, which should have a link to the state's geological survey or the U.S. Bureau of Mines. Ask around. Are there any mining or mineral shops nearby? Local rock clubs are a wealth of information. Do you know anyone who is into metal detecting? Talk to forest and park rangers. Does the river near you have lots of black sand on the bottom or rocks with a metallic sheen?

Once you find a river that has some history of gold discovery, you need to read the river for the spots where gold likes to hang out. Often in rushing rivers, the bedrock is exposed along streambeds and shorelines. The cracks in the bedrock are where gold tends to pile up and get trapped. As you watch the river flow, look for areas where the water slows down, such as the bottom of a rapid or a bend in the river. Gold is often found at the edges of whirlpools, and sometimes gold streaks can be found on sandbars. Also, look for obstructions, places where a ledge or a big boulder juts out and the water has to move around it.

EQUIPMENT

Panning for gold doesn't require fancy or expensive equipment, and if you go to a river known for its gold production, chances are there will be a store where you can rent the pans and shovels you need. Keep in mind that you will be knee deep in water for a good chunk of time, so a good pair of water shoes or waders might be helpful. Sneakers you don't mind getting wet are ideal because they have better traction than water shoes.

The most essential piece of equipment for gold panning is the pan. Some people use a pie plate or a frying pan. But these days, most prospectors use a plastic pan with a series of ridges or "riffles" on one side. The average-size pan has a 12 to 14-inch-wide bottom. The plastic pan is

lightweight, durable, and is usually a color that provides a sharp contrast to the gold, such as dark green or black.

A small shovel or trowel is important to dig away bigger rocks and get deeper into the hidden gold stores. But remember to be gentle as you dig. The bottoms of rivers are homes to many small creatures, so try not to disturb too much of their environment in your quest for the nuggets.

A glass vial is necessary to collect all of your gold flakes, and some people like to use a pair of tweezers to put these flakes into their vials so they don't fly or drift away.

As always, bring your keen mind, strong hands, and a curious heart, and, as prospector Sam Raddy says, "Grab your equipment and let the gold times roll!"

HOW TO PAN FOR GOLD

The most important fact to understand as you begin your prospecting adventures is that gold is very heavy — even heavier than lead. This is important because when you are filtering the water and sand out of your pan, the gold will be the last thing remaining on the very bottom of your pan. As renowned gold prospector C.J. Stevens says, "Let the weight of the gold work for you, and never forget that gravity is your friend!"

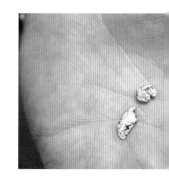

Step 1

Pick some promising material to work and fill your pan about halfway. Always pan in still or slowly moving water that is about one foot deep.

Step 2

Break up the material as if you are kneading dough and pull apart any materials that cling together, such as chunks of clay.

Step 3

Once the "pay dirt" is loosened up, swirl the pan in a circular motion and then shake it side to side. Make sure your pan is held flat and under water. Stevens suggests shaking the pan back and forth like a person shaking their head to say no—to settle the gold at the bottom.

Step 4

Pick the bigger rocks out and throw them back into the water.

Step 5

Place the side of your pan with the ridges away from you and tilt it toward the water about 10 degrees. Most of the pan should be under water. When you raise the pan, the spilling action of the water will pull the layer of lighter dirt over and out of the pan.

Step 6

The material left in the pan (about a couple of

tablespoons) will be the heaviest—black sand, pink garnets, and, hopefully, gold! Pull the pan out of the water, but make sure there is still about an inch of water left in the pan. Tilt the pan slightly and swirl to see if you can spot any shiny bits. Place the pan in the water one last time, shaking it gently and swirling to get the remaining sand out. Be careful, because if you are too rough with your shaking, you might lose precious gold flakes. Drain out the rest of the water and see if any tiny flakes of gold are hanging out on the bottom just waiting for you! If so, get out your tweezers and place them in your vial.

Repeat as necessary!

If on the first day of panning you walk away from the river with pockets full of gold nuggets, chances are that some of it might have fooled you. Pyrite, also known as fool's gold, and mica have a strong resemblance to gold and are plentiful in gold-producing rivers but have major structural differences. First, both pyrite and mica are lighter than gold, so they won't stay on the bottom of your pan. And if you hit pyrite and mica with a hammer, they will shatter, but gold will flatten. Once

you have sifted the fool's gold from the gold, you can take what's left and yell "eureka" all the way to the bank! ☠

Lifelong Gold Panner
Rosey Sudbury

When did you start panning for gold?

I was raised on the Swift River and had a pan in my hand when I was too young to know what to do with it other than chase baby fish around in the shallow water. I would say I was around five or six when I started pulling my own gold out of a pan.

What was your best find?

My best find was a pennyweight, which is 24 grains or 1/20th of an ounce (480 grains per ounce, 24 grains per pennyweight, 20 pennyweight per ounce.) It kind of looks like a bunny rabbit from a side profile, with his ears layed back. My husband was much luckier and found a ¾-ounce nugget — huge and heavy for here.

Do you have any advice for kids just starting out?

Gold is hard to find, so don't get your hopes up too much. Just plan to go and have a fun time looking for it and learning the process, and if you are lucky enough to find some it will be a bonus. Often it takes several attempts before you start finding gold.

Do you have any tricks or insider tips that you are willing to share?

I often tell people to just walk along the river until you find a spot that "just feels right." Also, expect to pan a lot of gravel and don't give up too quickly. Gold panning is like finding a needle in a haystack. You can move a lot of hay before you find the needle, or you might get lucky and find the needle right off!

One Person's Trash Is Another Person's Treasure

Metal Detecting

There is no beep more thrilling than the steady thrum of a metal detector alerting you to potential treasure, a sound about a million times better than that alarm clock waking you for school! Holding a metal detector is a little like holding a magic wand, one that can read the earth and dig deep within to find remnants of the past. Maybe you've seen people roaming up and down beaches with a metal detector extending from their arm and thought about giving it a try. Or maybe your grandparents gave you one for your birthday and you have used it only to find some old nails and then left it leaning against the garage. If you were given one, be thankful because many people call a metal detector the gift that keeps on giving. Now is the time to let your metal detector guide you to treasure and an entire lesson in history.

WHAT IS A METAL DETECTOR?

The metal detector was first invented by Alexander Graham Bell, the same guy who invented the telephone in the late 1800s. Basically, a metal detector uses radio waves to detect the presence of metal. The detector has a coil, similar to an antenna, and through this a radio signal is sent out, generating an electromagnetic field. When this electromagnetic line meets metal, detection occurs. Hence the beep. Most standard detectors can pick up a coin-size target that is six to nine inches deep. But the beep, according to master metal detector Glenn Leach, is not always the same, and experience will teach you the distinct language of your machine. As he says, "You've got to

understand first what the machine is telling you. Metal detectors can talk, but you've got to learn to listen to them. Signals sound different over a coin or a bottle cap, and there is no sound like a piece of gold. Old toys, musket balls, rings — they all have their voices." As you be-gin your quest, you need to become one with your machine. Read the instruction manual carefully and trust that the detector won't lie; it will report exactly what it finds.

WHAT TYPE OF DETECTOR SHOULD YOU BUY?

The big questions to ask before investing in a metal detector are what are you going to do with it and how often will you use it. There are metal detectors that cost more than $2,000 and have tons of features. Some people detect underwater and so there are special machines for that purpose. Some people use ones called "two box detectors" when they need to look deep in the ground for veins of gold, valuable meteorites, or deeply buried treasures. But chances are if you are just starting out or making a casual hobby of this, you will be fine with a reasonably priced basic model.

Once you have your machine, read the instruct-ion manual very carefully. Twice, or even better, three times. Once you have thoroughly digested everything about your detector, you need to stock your shelves with a ton of persistence. That is the name of the game. You might hear a lot of beeps but still not find one piece of metal even after you have learned to adjust the sensitivity settings on your instrument. Natural iron is found in much of the earth's soil and sometimes this will emit a signal and throw you off course. But the first time you find a rare coin, a wedding ring, or an old spoon is a thrill that will keep you on the hunt. As Glenn Leach puts it, "With treasure hunters there is an excitement of what is still to be found, the sharp edge of joy when finding it, and the memory of how it all happened." Finding an amazing treasure can happen to any-one at any time. This is what will keep you going. Just like the amateur metal detector who found the largest gold nugget ever, The Hand of Faith Nugget, which sold for one million dollars!

WHERE TO START METAL DETECTING

The easiest place to start metal detecting is in your own backyard. You never know what treasures await right outside your door. Investigating your own yard will give you hours of practice with your machine. And if you get thirsty, you can just head into your kitchen and get a drink. There actually could be treasure in your yard. Remember how we talked about the people who distrusted banks and preferred to bury their life savings in a secret spot in their yards. Maybe they passed on before ever telling anyone where that spot was, and today that tin can of coins is still buried, maybe near your house? On a smaller scale, your mom, or other moms who might have lived at your house before you did, might

have lost rings or earrings while gardening and have waited for your metal detector to uncover them!

If you live near the coast, a beach is a great spot to metal detect and is a close second to your backyard for learning the ropes of your machine. All summer long earrings are lost, coins slip out of pockets, rings fall in the sand, and all of these things can be recovered by you. There is a line at the beach known as "the treasure line." Some people also call it a "wrack line." You know that part of beach where all the rocks, shells, and seaweed get piled up? It is where the soft sand and the pebble-size rocks meet. After storms, this line is especially ripe for the picking, and many rings and coins will make their way to this special

spot. Another good beach spot is any area where sand has been eroded by rainwater runoff or strong surf. You see, below every sandy beach is a substrate of clay called hardback, and since gold is so heavy, it always sinks easily through the soft sand and down to the hardback. Next time your family packs up for the beach, don't forget your metal detector and head straight to the treasure line.

If you live in an old house, near a historic village, or in a place that has traditional stonewalls nearby, you are in for a metal-detecting history lesson. Before garbage trucks and town dumps, people threw their garbage out in the backyard. So somewhere on many properties across the country there are bottle dumps where the glass was thrown as well as old silver utensils, metal buttons, old toys, horseshoes, and more. These old home sites are treasure troves for metal detectors, but you must think like a historical detective. Where was the clothesline where the upside-down drying pockets filled with coins hung? Where was the path to the barn and the path from the well to the kitchen? Think about these paths and how many times a day the former inhabitants must have gone back and forth doing chores. What were these people like? If you pull something out of the ground that belonged to someone two hundred years ago, you are now connected to them. This thing that no one knew about or remembers losing is now yours. Treasure hunter Richard Carney Jr. says that, "Whatever you find here and keep will become a piece of your life just as it witnessed the passing of other lives. By lifting this from the earth you carry it into the future."

OTHER PLACES TO METAL DETECT

Parks and playgrounds

Showgrounds

Ghost towns

School yards

Picnic areas

Gold-mining sites

Camping grounds

Sports grounds

Swimming pool areas

Ski slopes in spring and summer

Plowed fields

Riverbanks

TECHNIQUE

The best metal detectors employ a slow and steady approach, searching the ground in a patient pattern. This is called sweeping. The key to sweeping is to move the coil on your detector very slowly while keeping it parallel to the ground at all times. The motto in the detectors' world is to "go slow and low". If you swing too fast, you will miss key targets. Experts recommend following a grid pattern to make sure you have covered every section of the hunting area. And when you find a hot spot, sweep very slowly to target the exact location and then make an X with your foot or use a stick to mark it.

HOW TO DIG FOR YOUR TREASURE

The last thing your parents want when they give you a metal detector is for you to dig up the whole yard whenever you hear a beep. Making plugs is the correct way to dig for treasure. This operation requires the use of a sharp knife, so adults should be on hand to help and supervise. A plug is a piece of earth that is about an inch square. Cut the ground with the knife and gently pull the square of earth up. Feel around in the dirt for the metal your detector alerted you to. It helps to carry a handkerchief, so you can scoop some of the dirt out and sift through it without making a mess. Once you find it, gently place the plug back in the ground. This technique works best in wet ground. If there hasn't been much rain lately, carry a

water bottle with you and pour it over the ground. Or if there is a hose nearby, soak the area first before you dig. This way your yard won't look like a bunch of moles had a party and your parents might actually be excited about the old nail that you found!

Another favorite technique of detectorists is using a small hand-held probe that kind of looks like a screwdriver with a worn-down tip. They use this probe to gently poke around the soil to feel for coins and other small objects. An experienced

Stay True to the Code

Just as there is a proper way to dig for treasure, there are ethics that go along with the hobby. The following is the Detectorist's Code of Ethics from The Task Force for Metal Detecting Rights Foundation.

- I will follow all laws relating to metal detecting on federal and state lands, as well as any laws pertaining to local areas I may be searching.

- I will respect private property and obtain the owner's permission before metal detecting.

- I will recover targets in a way that will not damage or kill vegetation and I will fill in holes completely, leaving the area looking as it was.

- I will remove all trash found and dispose of it properly.

- I will report discovery of any items that have significant historical value to the proper authorities.

- I will use common courtesy and common sense at all times.

- I will set a good example of how people should enjoy the lawful hobby of recreational metal detecting.

hunter will be able to tell whether the object underground is just a rock or a metal object they have detected, and often whether it is a coin, a ring, or a pull tab. Rumor has it that some old timers can tell you what kind of coin is underground and the date of it just by feeling it with their probe! Once they have established what it is, then they gently work it toward the surface and pop it out of the ground. This way they can detect all day and not dig one single hole.

It is helpful to carry a few small waterproof containers to put small treasures in that you find while hunting. A few cottonballs placed inside will keep delicate valuables from banging around and getting damaged.

HOW TO CLEAN YOUR TREASURES

Many of the items that you pull from the ground will be coated in dirt and will hopefully be very old. It is important not to wash the items that look really old immediately because the water might wash the surface of the object off. For example, if you find an old coin and wash it, you might wash away the date. The trick that expert metal detectorists use is to soak their finds in olive oil for a few days, then use an old toothbrush to gently scrub the dirt off, then soak it for another day or two. Olive oil works a bit like glue to stick things back together again.

As you go forth on the metal-detecting path, remember my advice about persistence. Not every day will be a great treasure-finding day, but there is always tomorrow. When Glenn Leach doesn't find anything, he says,

> *"Then I will find it tomorrow or the day after that. There is always that next signal. It isn't the idea that I want to find more than I already have. It's like the grab bags I used to buy when I was a kid. It wasn't the prize; it was what could be in that bag. So when the metal detector goes off, that's the same thing. I know it's something good. Darn, it's only an old rusty nail! But the next signal is going to be something. This is the way I go at it. And that's the sport."*

So good luck scanning the earth for metal, and may each beep lead you deeper into a connection with the past. As you dig up these metallic remains, you are a living example of the old saying, "one person's trash is another person's treasure." ☠

1491

Aaron Marcy: A Treasure-Hunting Life

I started metal detecting when I was still a child, probably six or seven. My father bought an inexpensive toy detector for me and my brother. They were very simple machines — you just turned them on and you were off, but they worked. So we were out in the remote hills of northern Tennessee digging up horseshoes and buffalo nickels and leaving a pockmarked landscape of holes as we went. Finally, our parents told us to fill in our holes. Always fill in your holes.

I grew up steeped in treasure hunting. Our whole family walked the freshly plowed tobacco fields every spring and fall, looking for Native American artifacts. We came home every day with arrowheads, spearheads, pottery, and fossils. I had a really cool fossil collection when I was a kid — enormous dinosaur bones and petrified wood and a snake fossilized into the top of a flat stone! The adults told amazing stories of people finding gold nuggets or buried money from train robberies, and us youngsters spent our days dreaming of finding these things. We were out there every day looking. My uncle Rex even took us gold panning in Georgia a few times. Treasure hunting is in my blood. I was always looking down at the ground for a stray coin or artifact lost or discarded a hundred years ago.

The Civil War belt buckle I found on North Haven Island in Maine is one of my favorite finds. I was detecting along an old stone wall in a large field and

I started finding old liquor bottles, harmonica parts, and tobacco tins, all from the mid-1800s. Everything was really close to the surface because there was no buildup of the decomposing material that buries objects in the forest. Then I got this really strong signal and I found a beautiful brass buckle shaped like a wreath, with the old leather still hanging from one end. I kept swinging my detector and soon found the other half of the brass buckle — it's called a tongue-and-wreath buckle, and was popular in the mid-1800s. The second piece, the part called the "tongue," had a gorgeous image of a fouled anchor on it (an anchor with a rope around it), so I assumed it was some sort of Naval buckle. I researched it for a long time, and eventually a collector in Hawaii told me it was from the Civil War era, but actually came off of a German sailor's uniform! Imagine, a German sailor 150 years ago on North Haven! I really like the story of this find, because it covers so many important aspects of metal detecting: the excitement of exploring remote locations, the thrill of discovery, the historical research, and the speculation of possible events. Was he a German sailor? Why was he on North Haven? What was he doing way out in that remote field, behind a large stone wall? Were the liquor bottles his? Was he alone? How did he lose his belt buckle?

I hope to return to the spot to do some more detecting, and maybe that will answer some of my questions. Until then, my imagination will have to take care of the rest.

Hide and Seek
Geocaching and Letterboxing

ith clues, a trail to follow, a creed, and even some Harry Potter terminology, geocaching is the latest treasure-hunting craze. Geocaching started in 2000 as an offshoot of letterboxing, which we discuss farther on in this chapter. With more than six million geocachers world-wide hitting the trail in search of some 2.25 million active geocaches, this hobby is truly taking the world by storm. There is even a geocache in space! So what is all the fuss about, and what exactly is geocaching? Anyone who has ever found a cache while holding a handheld GPS unit can speak to the suspense, the thrill, and the treasure awaiting at the end. The word "geo" means earth, and the word "cache" (pronounced cash) means a place for hiding things. Which means you will be exploring the earth for hidden containers bearing treasure. Caches are what explorers, gold miners, and pirates have used for centuries to hide their loot. In this case, the cache is hidden at a certain set of coordinates, the specific point that locates a position on a map. The cache is filled with cool trinkets and a log book to sign. But how exactly will you find this hidden cache?

The first step is to register at one of the many geocache websites, such as geocaching.com. To do this part you will need access

to the Internet. You will also need a hand-held GPS unit. GPS stands for global positioning system, which means the unit is able to give you your exact position in longitude and latitude coordinates at all times.

Once you register on-line, you will need to choose a special geocaching name for yourself, like "Raider of the Lost Cache" or "The Cache Kid" or even "Mad Dog." Provide your zip code and all of a sudden a list of every geocache

located in your area will pop up. You might be surprised that there are caches located in places you go all the time! As you look at the list of nearby geocaches, you will see that they are rated on a five-star scale based on how difficult they are to find and how challenging the terrain — 1 star is the easiest and 5 is the hardest. You will also learn how far away the cache is, the size and type, when it was placed, and when it was last found. And last but not least, you will see a clue. Many geocache clues are in code like this:

DECRYPTION KEY

A	B	C	D	E	F	G	H	I	J	K	L	M
N	O	P	Q	R	S	T	U	V	W	X	Y	Z

(Letter above equals letter below, and vice versa)

Or the clue might be a riddle. Whatever form the clue comes in, decipher it and write it down. If your parents have a smartphone, you can download a geocaching app that will have all of this information to bring with you on your hike. The app will even guide you to the cache. Note:

Do not rely solely on the smartphone app, or on your smartphone's GPS, to find the geocache because, depending on where you go, cell phone signals can be confused or weak, especially in dense forests or on top of high mountains.

Once you've chosen the geocache you want to locate, it's time to get ready for your adventure. Sometimes you will find the geocache quickly and easily, while other times it might take all day. Prepare for the second reality. Pack a backpack with water, snacks, an extra layer of clothing, sunscreen, bug spray, a map of the area, your GPS device, and, most importantly, a compass. Even with your GPS, you might still need help finding your way. The last thing to pack is a small treasure to leave in the geocache. An important rule in geocaching is if you take a treasure, you must leave something of equal or greater value. John McKinney, author of *Let's Go Geocaching*, says, "Remember the golden rule, leave for others what you'd like others to leave for you."

TYPES *of* CACHES
Excerpted from *Let's Go Geocaching!*

MICRO CACHE: Very small, film canister size.

SMALL CACHE: Small box, about the size of the tins that mints come in.

STANDARD: A plastic food container or a metal can.

LARGE: Can be as big as a five-gallon bucket.

MULTI: This cache has two or more finds, each with clues that direct you to a treasure.

VIRTUAL: A place without a hidden object.

WEBCAM CACHE: Coordinates send you to a public webcam, such as a park entrance or a bridge, then the webcam takes a picture to record your find.

The stuff inside a geocache is called SWAG, which stands for "stuff we all get." Examples of good geocache swag are small toys, crystals, key chains, bracelets, or outdoor gear like carabiners. Never leave trash, food, things you found on the trail like pine cones or rocks, or broken toys. Another good rule from John McKinney is "if you can't bring it to school, don't leave it in a geocache." No knives or firecrackers!

Once you are packed and ready, with your GPS, coordinates, and your clue — onward! However, only when you arrive at the coordinates does the hunt truly begin. Think about the clue, then look up, down, and around every square foot within about 16-20 feet of the coordinates. Geocaching.com warns that "geocaches are hidden in plain sight and

never buried, but they are often very cleverly camouflaged." This part of the hunt can be tricky and now is when you need all of your powers of observation, persistence, and stick-to-it-iveness. As one of my young friends said about this part of the hunt, "I wanted to give up and not give up at the same time." Sometimes you feel like you are going in circles and most likely you are. I have circled within five feet of a geocache for more than two hours before screaming, "I found it, I really found it." In that particularly tricky case, the cache was designed to look like a rock, so it blended in with the other rocks it was wedged under.

After you find the cache and have a "eureka" moment, reign it in and look around. Are there other people nearby casually enjoying their hike and not geocaching? If so, button it up. Those bystanders are known in geocaching circles as geo-muggles. Remember that word "muggles" from Harry Potter, meaning people who are unable to use magic? Try to be discreet so the geo-muggles don't come over and potentially move the cache from its coordinate location.

The reward of a well-found geocache is an actual reward. Dig into the cache and see what goodies await. Don't forget to put the treasure you brought inside, and make sure you sign the logbook with your name, the date, and any notes that you want to share. Some caches even have a camera so you can take your picture! After you have explored the contents of the cache, put everything back in, seal it, and place it exactly where you found it so the next round of geocachers can enjoy it the way you have. In fact, that is one of the guiding principles in the Geocacher's Creed:

WHEN PLACING OR SEEKING GEOCACHES, I WILL:

- Not endanger myself or others.
- Observe all laws and rules of the area.
- Respect property rights and seek permission if needed.
- Avoid causing disruptions.
- Minimize impact on the environment.
- Be considerate of others and animals.
- Preserve and care for other people's caches.

Another important rule, despite not being in the official creed, is "Cache In, Trash Out," known simply as CITO. This rule pretty much goes without saying, but the point is to leave the area where you are geo-

caching better than how you found it. Keep the scene clean so geocachers don't get a bad reputation.

After you've been geocaching for a while, you might decide to join the more than two million caches by creating your own. Making your own cache is pretty simple. You will need some sort of waterproof container, a log book placed in a plastic bag, and treasures. Once you have filled your cache, mark the outside clearly as a geocache so nobody mistakes it for trash or steals it. Find a site for your geocache. If you are thinking about planting it in a state or city park, or on someone's private property, make sure that you seek permission. Once you have been given the go-ahead, bring your GPS and find the exact coordinates of your hidey-hole. Think of a name for your cache that ties in with what makes it unique. Write a brief description of the geocache and come up with a clue to help people find it, but not too easily. Remember that geocache I told you about that looked like a rock The clue was "Granite or not?"

Geocaching Friends

What was your best geocache day?

Hunter: *The best geocache day was when we went to Rangeley Memorial weekend 2013. We went with a group of family members in three cars and drove around Rangeley in the pouring rain wearing rain ponchos. That day we found seven geocaches! One was in an old phone booth and one was on a shoe nailed to a telephone pole!*

Haden: *My favorite geocaching day was when we were on Nantucket. We had written down a few to find so if we found one we didn't have to stop. One of them was a small container that was disguised as a screw on the underside of a bench.*

What makes a good geocache?

Hunter: *Having family and friends with you and discovering new places. Trading trinkets is fun, too!"*

Haden: *A good geocaching day is made by having your family with you. If it is too hard it is not fun because you can't find it or are discouraged."*

Do you have any tips for those just starting out?

Hunter: *Use the hints that the person who left the geocache gives you. Most important, don't give up. We couldn't find one once and went back and found it the next time with the help of my big brother Levi!*

Haden: *The best way to start out is by looking on the website for a relatively easy geocache. Also a GPS specific for coordinates is very helpful."*

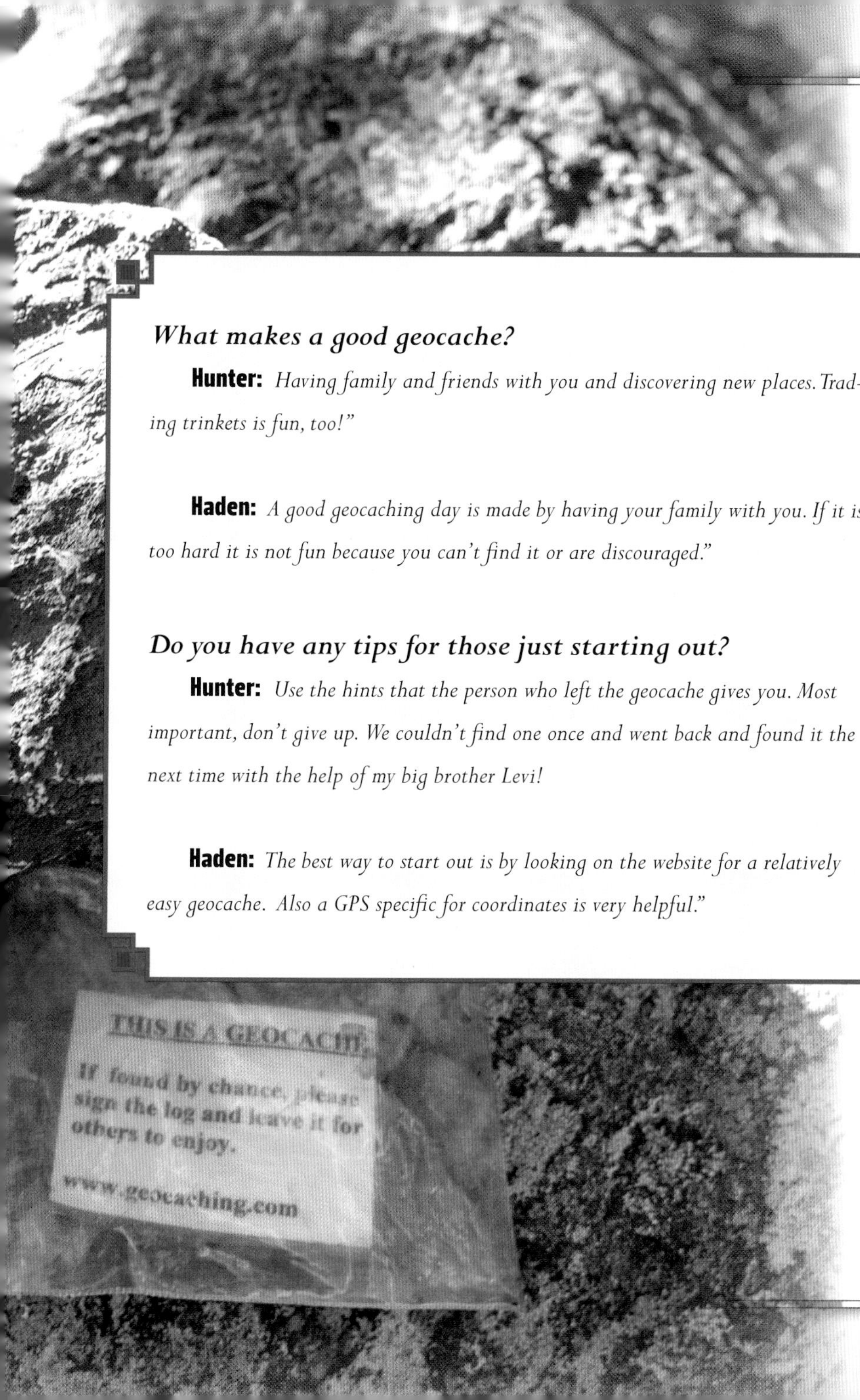

THIS IS A GEOCACHE.

If found by chance, please sign the log and leave it for others to enjoy.

www.geocaching.com

163I

Once you have written all of these components and received your parents' permission, you can now add the cache to a geocaching website. Once it is posted don't forget to keep up with your cache. See how many people have visited. Check it once in a while to see who's signed your log and what treasures they left and to refill the treasures you want people to take with them. And always remember to keep up the good hunt!

LETTERBOXING

If you like the idea of geocaching but are looking for something a bit more artsy and a little less technological, you might find geocaching's older cousin, letterboxing, up your alley. Letterboxing works a lot

like geocaching — a water-proof container is hidden in an interesting, remote, or beautiful place, such as on a mountain top or at a nature center. The hider of the letterbox creates a clue that might range from puzzling to poetic. These clues are entered and compiled online at letterboxing.org or atlasquest. com and listed according to geographic area.

The difference between geocaching and letterboxing is that the letterbox contains a rubber stamp and a logbook, and the person hunting for the letterbox carries a rubber stamp with them. It is this stamping element that separates the two treasure hunts. The rubber stamp can either be made from scratch or store-bought, but it should somehow convey the personality of the hunter. Letterbox enthusiasts take great pride in their rubber stamp designs, and many make them themselves. It is this element of the hobby that gives it a more creative and crafty feel.

If searching for letterboxes in your hometown or while on vacation, be equipped with a pen or pencil, your unique stamp, a stamp pad, and a personal logbook. Log books, similar to stamps, can be decorated prior to the hunt, providing yet another creative element to this endeavor. Once the clue is deciphered and the box is found, you simply stamp the logbook held within the box with your stamp and then stamp your logbook with the stamp inside the letterbox. This stamped record grows in your logbook and becomes a vibrant visual representation of all the letterboxes you've discovered.

Letterboxing hasn't always relied on this element, and the history of this activity is as colorful as the stamped markings in a full logbook.

The first letterbox was not a box at all, but a bottle placed in 1854 by a man named James Perrott in a very remote and inaccessible area of the moors in Dartmoor, England. Perrott placed his calling card in the bottle so people would be able to contact him and leave their own information. The hike to this difficult terrain was momentous, and the few people who made the trek proudly added their cards to the bottle, thus beginning the hobby we know today as letterboxing. The bottle was replaced by a tin in 1888, followed in 1905 by a logbook. In this very logbook, a man named John H. Strother suggested adding a rubber stamp to offer "proof" that people had really made it to this remote place. One hundred twenty-two years from the time Perrott placed his bottle, fifteen letterboxes were created and scattered throughout the moors in Dartmoor. A map was drawn and soon this slowly growing hobby caught fire. But not everyone was happy about the sudden letterbox explosion — in their quest, letterboxers began dismantling historic rock walls, leaving litter, and even painting graffiti markers to show the locations of letterboxes. Many officials in the area wanted to remove all the letterboxes and put an end to the hobby. But one man, Godfrey Swinscow, created the all-important letterboxing code of conduct that still guides hobbyists today:

1. Boxes should not be sited in any kind of antiquity, in or near stone rows, circles, cists, cairns, buildings, walls, ruins, peat cutters' or tinners' huts, etc.

2. Boxes should not be sited in any potentially dangerous situations where injuries could be caused.

3. Boxes should not be sited as a fixture. Cement or any other building material is not to be used.

With this code of conduct firmly in place, letterboxing remained in Dartmoor and then began to spread throughout the world due to a small article in *Smithsonian* magazine. According to the website atlasquest. com, "By 2001, over a thousand letterboxes dotted the United States, covering all 50 states. Letterboxers traveling to international locations started to plant letterboxes around the globe from Aruba to Zimbabwe."

Just as you might be surprised by how many geocaches can be found near your house, the same will be true for letterboxes. Places you never thought to visit will tempt you as you learn that they are home to a series of clues and letterboxes. On vacation, you may get to know new territory better by exploring it through letterboxing. Not only will you have a chance to explore the world around you, but you will leave your own creative stamp behind, marking the spot forever.

How to Make a Rubber Stamp

Put some newspaper down on a large, flat workspace. Cut a small square out of the Speedy-Carve, roughly 2 inches by 2 inches.

Think about a design that is unique to you or just something you love. Practice drawing this a few times before drawing it on your square. Remember that if you are carving a word, you will need to carve it backwards. Also, whatever you carve will not pick up ink when stamping, it is the flat areas that will hold the ink.

Once you are happy with your design, begin carving. Carve away from your body and have adult supervision. Take very small, careful strokes as you dig out your image.

Glue your finished design onto the piece of wood and let it dry.

Practice stamping your design and see how it looks on paper. You can keep fine-tuning your design until you get it right.

When you are finished, wrap the stamp in a piece of square felt and bind it with a rubber band to absorb any extra ink.

SUPPLIES:

A sheet of Speedball Speedy-Carve: It's pink and available at craft stores

A gouge chisel and an X-Acto knife

A piece of wood to mount your stamp

Glue

A pencil

A piece of scrap paper to practice your designs

Walking on Time
Hunting for Rocks and Minerals

o your coat pockets weigh ten pounds because you can't bear to leave any newly found rock specimens behind? Perhaps you have an entire drawer filled with rocks from different places you've traveled or a collection of crystals and mica that has grown since you were old enough to know not to throw rocks at your little sister or brother. Well, then this is the chapter you have been waiting for! According to a young geologist I know, holding a rock in the palm of your hand is like "holding a piece of time." However, questions immediately arise — what kind of rock is it, how old is it, and where did it come from? These questions form the basis of the scientific process, and by asking them you are following in the footsteps of geologists and earth scientists everywhere. Geology, the study of the origin, structure, and history of the earth, is a complicated field and people study it for their entire lifetimes. For our treasure-hunting purposes, we will glaze over the science, instead focusing on how to gather cool, perhaps even valuable, rocks and minerals and how to tell what they are.

The hobby of gathering rocks and minerals is known as rock hounding. Younger rock hounds are sometimes called "pebble pups," but basically you are hounding, like a dog, for rock and mineral specimens worthy of your collection. What is amazing about rock hounding is the incredible variety of colors, textures, and shapes that are created from the earth. That these glittering gems and bold specimens are pushed up through the ground is nothing short of magical. When you dig up a rock or a mineral, you are pulling something out of the earth that no one else has ever seen or touched. This unearthed treasure could very well be a valuable piece of jewelry. But keep in mind the advice from rock hound John Allen May, "It is a hobby without parallel . . . you may become rich but you are more likely to become happy."

WHAT ARE ROCKS AND MINERALS?

Here is a quick tutorial, otherwise known as the basics. Minerals are non-living solids found in nature and they form the basic building blocks of the earth. Scientists have identified more than four thousand different minerals. Minerals are everywhere around you. The talcum powder that your parents used on your diaper rash comes from a mineral. The handle-bars on your bicycle, the aluminum foil wrapped around your sandwich, the salt in your food, even your toothpaste, all come from minerals. Minerals have five defining characteristics: they must be a solid, must occur in nature, have a chemical composition, contain a crystalline structure, and be inorganic, which means they were never alive. When trying to determine the type of mineral found, mineralogists look at a number of different things, including the color, hardness, luster or shininess, the shape of the crystals, density, whether it is magnetic, and the cleavage, or the way that the mineral breaks. They also perform a streak test, which is the color of the mark, or streak, the mineral makes when you scrape it on a streak plate, which is basically a piece of unglazed porcelain.

Rocks are combinations of one or more minerals. All rocks fall into three categories: igneous, sedimentary, and metamorphic. Igneous rocks are made from magma and form as the magma

Mineral Scavenger Hunt Chart

Look for these minerals and mineral products at home, in school, at a pharmacy, or in a hardware store.

MINERAL OR MINERAL PRODUCT	USES
ALUMINUM	aluminum foil, cosmetics, beverage cans, deodorant, hand lotion, antacids, cooking pots
BERYLLIUM	fluorescent lamps
CHROMIUM	chrome fixtures (cars, bicycles, lamps, kitchens, etc.), stainless steel, copper wires, pipes, cooking pots, old gutters and roofs, brass, pennies
FLUORITE *(fluoride)*	toothpaste, drinking water
GOLD	dentistry, jewelry, computers, electronics
GYPSUM	wallboard, plaster
HALITE *(salt)*	table salt, food preservatives, de-icers
IRON	cosmetics, hair dye, steel, wrought iron
LEAD	car batteries, computers, fuel tanks, TV tubes, leaded glass, x-ray shields, fishing sinkers
MICA	sheetrock, paints, hair dye, cosmetics, soap, electronics

MOLYBDENUM	fertilizer, filament supports in light bulbs, steel
NICKEL	nickel coins, stainless steel, alnico magnets, sheetrock
PERLITE	gardening
PHOSPHATE	fertilizer, dishwashing detergent, laundry detergent
POTASSIUM *(potash)*	fertilizer, toothpaste
SILICA	computer chips, glass, cosmetics, antacids, paint, laundry detergent, drain cleaner, quartz watche
SILVER	photograph developing, jewelry, electronics, silverware, dentistry
SULFUR	fertilizers, matches, car tires
TALC	baby powder, cosmetics, antacids, sheetrock, primer
TITANIUM	cosmetics, hand lotion, soap, toothpaste, hair dye, bug spray, primer, paint
TUNGSTEN	filament in light bulbs, drill bits (tool steel)
ZINC	sunblock, fertilizer, cosmetics, dandruff shampoo, pennies, galvanized metal, brass, dry-cell batteries
ZIRCONIUM	deodorant, jewelry

cools and hardens. Granite is one of the most common igneous rocks.

Sedimentary rocks are created by layers of silt and rock particles being laid down one on top of another. Over millions of years the weight of the layers pushing down creates rock. The walls of the Grand Canyon are a great place to see what layers of sedimentary rock look like.

Metamorphic rocks may have started out as igneous or sedimentary rocks, but have been changed due to incredibly high amounts of heat or pressure. Slate is a kind of metamorphic rock that was made from the sedimentary rock shale; and marble is made from the sedimentary rock limestone.

All rocks break down at the surface of the earth from environmental factors like freezing and thawing, wind, and the flow of water. This is called the rock cycle because rocks continually recycle through these three stages. New rocks are formed every day and they are transformed and reshaped constantly.

What is the difference between a rock and a mineral? According to the United States Geological Survey, "A mineral is a naturally occurring, inorganic compound with a unique chemical structure and physical properties. A rock is a solid, stony mass composed of a combination of minerals or other organic compounds. For example, quartz and feldspars are minerals, but when formed together, they make the rock granite."

GEMSTONES

One of the most distinguishing properties of a mineral is its ability to
form exquisite crystals. Gemstones are the most prized of these beau-
ties. Thinking about gemstones immediately calls to mind diamond
rings, the Queen of England's crown, and other sparkly pieces of jewelry. But uncut gems are often not as fancy as you might think. They are
actually rather ordinary looking. It is when they are cut and polished
that they turn into jeweled treasures. Gemology is an entire branch of
science that studies gems. Gemologists determine the quality of gems,
and classify them into their different groups based on their properties

and chemical structure. Gemstones are divided into semi-precious and precious, with diamonds, rubies, sapphires, and emeralds leading the charge among precious gems. Diamonds are the hardest natural substance found on earth and are made of carbon atoms. Rubies and sapphires are created from the base mineral corundum. Emeralds are from the mineral beryl, which is one of the most important gem varieties. Semi-precious amethysts are from quartz; and here in Maine, there's an abundance of a beautiful semi-precious gem called tourmaline, which is found readily mixed with quartz rocks.

HOW TO FIND ROCKS AND MINERALS

Just as there are millions of rocks, there are millions of places to find them. Rock hounds most often look at the following places: outcrops, where bare rocks stick up out of the ground; abandoned quarries or mines; paths next to rivers and streams; along the bottoms of really steep hills; and on rocky beaches at low tide. The most important rule when digging for gems and minerals is to get permission if you are planning to visit a mine on private or state-owned land. Often joining a mineralogical society is a good way to gain access to restricted places that are filled with mine trailings and other mineral deposits. These groups take field trips, and when you join you are invited to go along and learn from experts who have been rock hunting for many years. Look

online at your state's Bureau of Land Management and you will find links to geological surveys. There might be old quarries in your town that are open to the public and, with an adult to accompany you, these are great places to begin a rock hunt. If you live in an area with mountains, then hiking will lead you to a literal minefield of rocks and minerals — on a mountain in our town, we found a valuable gem known as garnet schist. The key to a successful day rock hounding is to do a little research and make sure you go to an area that has a plethora of . . . you guessed it, rocks! Author Jean Blakemore says to find a hopeful rock-hunting spot, look for a place where things look all mixed up like bread pudding." At this pudding site, get out your shovel and begin digging. Rock hounds recommend that you dig two to three feet deep to hit what is known as pay dirt, which means ground that contains rocks and minerals in a large enough quantity to be worth pulling out — again, always remember to get permission from the landowner before digging large holes on their property.

Don't forget one of the number one spots for rock hunting is the beach. Beaches are great for rock hunting because of the variety of churned, eroded, sedimentary rocks to be found. The layering of sedimentary rocks makes them particularly good for what is known as lapidary, which means they can be sliced and polished into gemstones. One example of a shore-side find is agate. When looking for agate, you will see that it has a waxy, banded appearance. When you crack agate open with a rock hammer, the inside will be a banded geode.

WHAT TO BRING ON A ROCK HUNT

- ⊕ Clothing: Wear what you would normally wear on a hike, but always bring some warm clothes and a raincoat in case the weather changes.
- ⊕ Food and water
- ⊕ Prospector's pick
- ⊕ Rock hammer
- ⊕ Shovel
- ⊕ Compass
- ⊕ Magnifying glass
- ⊕ Flashlight
- ⊕ Plastic bags — on each bag write the name of the mineral, date, and where collected
- ⊕ United States Department of Interior Geological Survey maps showing the area you plan to visit
- ⊕ Protective goggles
- ⊕ Gloves

Gem and mineral books can be left in the car — if you see anything at all interesting on your hunt, grab it and identify it later. The books, while important, will just weigh you down.

SAFETY WHILE COLLECTING ROCKS

Always collect with an adult. Wear safety goggles as well as gloves when cracking open or break-ing rocks with your pick or rock hammer. Do not climb on danger-ous ledges, crumbly rock walls, or quarry walls. Watch for falling rocks.

SCREENING FOR ROCKS AND MINERALS

Often rock and mineral stores will have mine trailings for sale from working mines that you can buy to take home and screen. These bags of trailings will come with an identification tag that describes the minerals by their color and are filled with a variety of rock and mineral speci-mens — a great way to build up your collection. When you get home, use a small window screen insert or use a staple gun to attach a piece of screening to an old frame. Pour a small portion of the bag contents onto the screen. Because mines are exploded with dynamite to release the minerals, the trailings are covered in dust, which you will need to rinse off. Dunk the screen carefully in a big tub of water to rinse off the dirt. Shake the contents of your screen gently and notice which ones are

{85}

shiny. Take out some of the bigger rocks and dip your screen back in the water to give it another rinse. Continue poring through until you have found all possible gems. Repeat the process until you have gone through the entire bag.

IDENTIFYING YOUR FINDS

The easiest way to identify what you've collected is to try and match it up with a picture from a rock and mineral book. Many websites have great photographs and identifying databases. Rockhounds.com has an interactive identification key.

If you're feeling adventurous, you could try to use some of the characteristics that professional mineralologists use, such as the luster, cleavage, or streak test. You'll need a good geology or minerology textbook, however, to be able to match up all the possible characteristics with your mineral.

OTHER WAYS TO EXPAND YOUR ROCK AND MINERAL KNOWLEDGE

Visit your state natural history museum and your local museums and study the exhibits of which rocks and minerals are abundant in your area. Many of these museums have a hands-on learning center where you can actually hold different rocks and really study them.

Visit a rock and mineral store. These stores are often chock-full of treasures and the owners are a wealth of knowledge. Rocks for Kids (rocksforkids.com) is a great website that sells reasonably priced rocks and can help you get your collection started.

Attend a gem and mineral show. The vendors at these shows are highly knowledgeable and at some shows there are even educational booths with activities to encourage young geologists.

Contact a local geological or a gem and mineral society. Some chapters have volunteers who can present at schools or community centers and they offer family membership rates. ☠

Found Treasures
Sea Glass, Fossils, Meteorites, and More

Some treasure hunts don't require a GPS or a metal detector because some treasures are best found by using your own two eyes while kicking around. Observation is the key to a life as a successful treasure hunter. Developing your treasure-hunting skills means sharpening your senses, especially your deep vision and your gut. The best treasure hunters work from feelings of intuition, which means that you just know something without really knowing why. Finding treasure is a lesson in paying attention. Once you get a taste for it, you will find treasure everywhere. One person I know found an ancient obsidian spearhead and someone else I know found a perfectly round sea glass marble. Once these treasures are uncovered, they then become part of a collection.

Treasure hunting and collecting go hand in hand. To a collector, anything that fits into their particular collection is a treasure. For example, a rubber band might be a treasure to someone because they are collecting them to make the world's largest rubber-band ball. I know collectors of sea shells, acorn caps, dried beetles, bottle caps, you name it. You can even start a collection of all the things from your geocaches, or the coins and nails from metal detecting. But some finds in nature are unique and call out to you as a bonafide treasure bonanza, especially rare items such as four-leaf clovers and sand dollars. These finds are known to carry good luck with them, probably because you were fortunate to find something not everyone else could. Many people take their found treasures and make them into art. Sea glass artists make jewelry, lamps, and trays out of their finds. Some people gather driftwood and polish it, turning it into sculptures and lamp bases. These art pieces made from collections then become part of other people's art collections.

The following are three examples of treasures that can be found just by using really good observation and hunting skills: sea glass, fossils, and meteorites. They are not always easy to find, but with practice and stick-to-it-iveness who knows what you will come up with.

SEA GLASS

If you've ever seen the glimmer of blue sea glass in the midst of a pile of shells, you will understand why sea glass collectors are so obsessed with their hunt. There is something mysterious about sea glass and its journey. Who knows if it is a piece of glass from a ship wreck hundreds of years ago or from a bottle dumped over the side of a boat carrying immigrants to America?

1911

Much of the very smooth, well-worn sea glass that people prize is indeed from these historic journeys and wrecks. These glass remnants are really pieces of old trash that have been shattered and flung about on the bottom of the sea and then washed up for eager collectors to find. Sea glass expert C.S. Lambert talks about this notion of garbage, which, "however unappealing, creates an unexpected variety of treasure — from porcelain doll fragments to chunks of crystal to a broken plate revealing an image that is nothing short of a miniature masterpiece."

There are certain prizes in sea glass collecting, and the rarest colors are valued the most. Deep purple, yellow, orange, red, black, turquoise, lavender, and blue are the rarest; while brown, white, and green are more readily available. The value of sea glass is dramatically increased if the glass comes from a handmade source as opposed to much more common production glass.

Sea glass enthusiasts have several tricks up their sleeves, but mainly they have a steady supply of patience and determination. Most collectors try to get to the beach about an hour before low tide to get a jump start on combing the beach. They generally like beaches that have pebbles and shells because that means there is a lot of movement and wave action. Expert sea glass collector Jacques Bouchard offers the following advice: "Take your time and move slowly — even if there is a lot of beach to cover. Let the sea glass 'jump out' at you as you stare at the sand. What we've learned over the years is that every beach has its own character and that the selection of colors you're likely to find can vary widely."

One sea glass enthusiast named Richard Carney doesn't wait for the sea glass to wash up on the shore, but instead dives under the water and finds all kinds of treasure. Here is an excerpt from an interview about his favorite finds that appeared in the *Working Waterfront:*

Two to three times a week, year-round, Richard Carney of Brunswick spends hours with his entire arm stretched into the mud of lake, river, or ocean waters. If he feels a bottle or something else, he brings it up. Sometimes, it can be quite a find, like an

unusual whole piece of crockery or an undam-
aged 1700s bottle. Sometimes he finds just the
one piece; other times there is a pile of the
same sort of artifact, like the numerous clay
pipes he found recently in New Hampshire.

Each dive is a new adventure. A man of
great enthusiasm, he admits that occasionally,
when he comes up with a special artifact or
locates a rich site, he will "get giggly underwa-
ter" and yell, "All right!"

Now 46, Carney has been diving for about
25 years, bringing home 2,000 to 5,000
items a year. He has kept some, sold many,
and turned others into crafts. Two years ago,
he added a sideline when he decided to do
something with the mounds of sea glass he
was pushing aside to reach the bottles and
other artifacts. "I had an epiphany," he says.
"Sell it."

Carney began collecting bottles when he was a kid living in
Buxton and in Winthrop, where he was close to a 1770s stage-
coach inn. He picked through land dumps of the inn and exist-
ing and defunct old farms. But those sources were scoured, he

says, during the "seventies bottle craze," and good finds became scarce.

He finds his sites in many ways, often using old maps and local lore. For one dive, he consulted an 1877 map of the South End of the City of Bath and Winnegance. Unrolling the map, he points to an area just beyond the causeway, where he says he's counted 49 houses perched above Winnegance Lake. Knowing from experience that residents living by the water in the 1800s often chucked what they didn't want out the windows on the water side, he figures the site is full of artifacts.

Other favorite sites are off old docks, like the town dock in Wiscasset. That location is loaded with wine and spirit bottles, the trash, he believes, from several 19th-century taverns in the town. It's one of his prime sources for sea glass. Another rich location is the site of an old stone pier across from Center Pond in Phippsburg. Picking up a bottle he found there, he shows that a name is visible: Hartlib & Shelter Soda Co., which he says was in Bath during the 1890s.

FOSSILS

Collecting fossils requires a lot of research mixed with even more luck. Becoming a fossil hunter or a paleontologist is a tall order, but many amateurs have stumbled upon very important and interesting fossil remains. The key to being a good fossil hunter is to learn about all different kinds of fossils, especially those that are common where you live. First, a little background: a fossil is the preserved remains of a plant or animal, but burrows and footprints can also be fossilized. Fossil remains create the evidence of 3.5 billion years of life, and by studying them, scientists get a view of what ancient life was like on earth. The process of fossilization takes place over millions of years and in that time only a tiny number of the specimens once alive make it into fossil form. Fossils are rare because for something to become a fossil it must be quickly buried and covered by dirt, sand, or mud.

Almost three hundred years ago, the first fossil hunting began in earnest. Today, paleontologists work all over the world to uncover fossils and learn more about ancient life on our planet. The range of fossils to discover is vast, but the following list covers some of the most common:

- Coral
- Shells: snails, clams, mussels, oysters
- Mollusks: ammonites, nautiloids
- Arthropods: crabs, insects, scorpions, lobsters, millipedes
- Echinoderms: starfish, sea urchins
- Fish: shark's teeth, fins, spines, skeletons
- Plants: ferns, horsetails

HOW TO FIND FOSSILS

Fossil hunting, like all treasure hunting, is about carefully observing the landscape around you, so your best tools are your eyes. Gazing over large areas of potential fossil grounds takes time and patience, and you still might only find one or two tiny fossils. As you get more experienced, it gets easier to know what you are looking for and the different characteristics that separate fossils from their surroundings. To be successful in this pursuit, you need to know what types of fossils are abundant in your area. Visit a local or state museum or write to them requesting information. Go to the library to research books on fossils and especially guidebooks for fossils in your region. Look online at your state's geological survey, which should have ample fossil information. Some

fossil-hunting sites are open to the public, but many require permission
prior to visiting and are protected, so you can go and look but you are
not allowed to take any of these home. Fossils are most readily abundant in sedimentary rocks such as limestone. Fossils can be found in
any areas where sedimentary rocks are exposed, so coastal beaches are
great targets, but so are quarries, farms, and even your own backyard.
Once you find a handful of fossils, you can start a collection. Look at

your fossils and compare them to pictures in books and fossils on exhibit. Write a label for each fossil, noting where you found it, what type of rock you think you found it in, and what you think it is. If you find a very large or significant fossil, you should notify someone of your find. Your discovery could shed light on our earth's evolution, just like the fossil Mary Anning found in 1810 when she was 11 years old.

MARY ANNING

Mary Anning was born on the coast of England in a town called Lyme Regis. Her father encouraged her interest in collecting

curiosities and she gathered many fossils that at that time had magical names like thunderbolts, fairy's hearts, crocodile's teeth, and devil's toenails. But her biggest find was wedged in the muddy cliffs — the complete skeleton of an ichthyosaur, which she carefully unearthed and thought

---

EQUIPMENT NEEDED *for* FOSSIL HUNTING

ROCK HAMMER

CHISELS

TROWELS

BRUSHES FOR BRUSHING AWAY DIRT DURING AN EXCAVATION

MAGNIFYING LENS

SIEVE FOR STRAINING AND SEPARATING SMALL FOSSILS

PLASTIC CONTAINERS FOR COLLECTING

Fossil Folklore

As we have learned more about ancient life, many of the theories that people once had about the fossils they found have been proven wrong, but they are quite fun to look back on. Before fossils were identified with scientific names, they carried whimsical names like snake stone and fairy's heart. For many years, fossil hunters believed the tusk of the small narwhal whale was the horn of a unicorn until mammoth tusks were discovered, and then they became known as unicorn horns. Another example of a fossil myth is from an extinct squid-like animal known as a belemnite. This fossil was believed to have medicinal powers because people thought they were flung from the heavens as "darts during a thunderstorm."

was a sea monster. It was one of the most important fossils ever found at that time, and young Mary began her career as the first woman paleontologist at the ripe age of 11. Throughout her life she found many more important finds, including two complete plesiosaurs and the first pterodactyl ever found in England. Mary's lifetime saw a shift in people's understanding of the world, 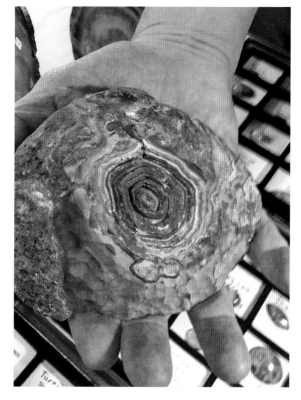 and her discoveries proved that the world was much older than anyone previously believed. Her interest in "curiosities" and a treasure-hunting spirit allowed a young girl to unearth these amazing fossils and make an impact on history. Perhaps you will follow in Mary Anning's footsteps!

ROCKS FROM SPACE

Did you know that every year about 19,000 meteorites fall to earth? While most fall into the ocean or are lost deep in the desert, some of these space rocks might land in a spot near you! Many people believe they have found a meteorite, but of all these hopefuls, less than 1% of strange, space-looking rocks are actually true meteorites. So how can you tell if that peculiar mass you found is a former star or just a piece of regular old rock? There are actually two easy ways to tell: the magnet test and the texture test.

Magnet Test: This test will determine if your specimen has iron in it, which is one of the key ingredients in a meteorite. Hang a magnet from a piece of string, a fridge magnet is fine, but a super-strong "rare earth" magnet is the best. Bring the rock to the magnet, not the magnet to the rock. If the rock is magnetic, chances are more likely that it is a meteorite, but not 100%. Many rocks have iron in them, such as hematite, so this is not a sure bet.

Texture Test: This is a test of observation. Meteorites are distinctive because of their "fusion crust," which is caused by the melting of the rock's surface as it enters our atmosphere. This thin black crust will begin to rust because of the meteorite's iron content, and so the color will turn reddish brown. Meteorites do not have bubbles or holes like lava

rock. Their features are smooth, but their surface is slightly rough.

If your meteorite passes these two tests, things are looking good that you are holding something that catapult- ed into our atmosphere, but it couldn't hurt to get an expert opinion before you start charging your neighbors 50 cents to see it. Meteorites are pretty special and there are people who spend all of their treasure-hunting time looking just for them. Perhaps after you find your first one, you will join these meteor- ite enthusiasts on a quest for space rocks.

Just imagine how cool it would be to hold a rock that blasted into our atmosphere from space.

THE FINAL CLUE

Treasure hunting is about appreciation and finding things around you that excite you and tell a story. The world is filled to the brim with trea- sures of all kinds, and it is up to you to find whatever treasure brings

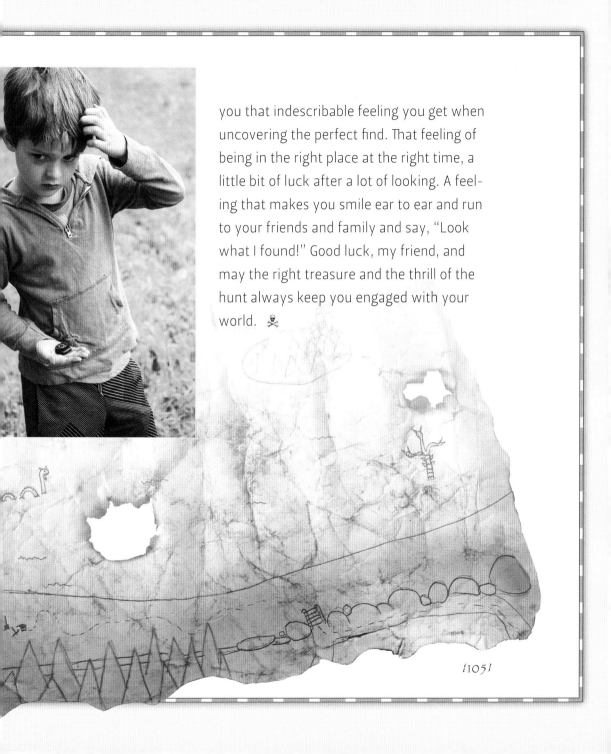

you that indescribable feeling you get when uncovering the perfect find. That feeling of being in the right place at the right time, a little bit of luck after a lot of looking. A feeling that makes you smile ear to ear and run to your friends and family and say, "Look what I found!" Good luck, my friend, and may the right treasure and the thrill of the hunt always keep you engaged with your world. ☠

Resources

Pirates

The True Tales of Pirates and Their Gold by Edward Rowe Snow

The Pirates Handbook by Margarette Lincoln

D.K. Eyewitness: Pirate by Richard Platt

The World of the Pirate by Val Garwood

Treasure Island by Robert Louis Stevenson

Lost Loot: Ghostly New England Treasure Tales by Patricia Hughes

Haunted New England: A Devilish View of the Yankee Past
      by Mary Bolte and photography by Mary Eastman

Gold Panning

The $3.25 How to Pan for Gold Book by Sam Radding

Coos Canyon Rock and Gift Store in Byron, Maine

Rocks and Minerals

D.K. Eyewitness: Rocks and Minerals by Dr. R.F. Symes

We Walk on Jewels: Treasure Hunting in Maine for Gems and Minerals by Jean Blakemore

Smithsonian Education: smithsonianeducation.org

Fossils:

D.K. Eyewitness: Fossils by Paul Taylor

Stone Girl, Bone Girl by Laurence Anholt

Mary Anning and the Sea Dragon by Jeannine Atkin

Acknowledgements

I have always loved treasure hunts and writing often feels like a quest with a series of clues hopefully pointing in the right direction. This book was guided by many people who provided the right tip at exactly the right time. Thank you first to Michael Steere for putting me on the map, listening to my ideas, and having endless amounts of patience and humor. Lynda Chilton continues to amaze me with her inspired designs and style. Jennifer Smith-Mayo captured all the moments on the hunt with such gorgeous photographs while also taking on the role of camp counselor! Terry Bregy and Linda Callahan continually save the day and are the super heroes who get the book into the hands of the people.

I learned a variety of new information while writing this book and couldn't have gotten very far without the sage advice of so many experts.

Thank you to Rosie Sudbury, Aaron Marcy, Brad LaRoche, and Richard Carney. Thank you to Hunter Crabtree and Haden Wikar for their geocaching insight. Mr. LaRoche's class let me sit in and listen to their amazing rock discoveries: Mason, Danila, Nick, Tanner C., Logan, Montana, Robert, Caleb, Tanner H., Joel, Sam, Shannon, Noah, Molly, Annabel P., Abby,

Joshua, Zaid, Phoebe, Benjamin, Gage, Annabelle W., and Michael. Ava and Luke Tobias, and William and Bennett Gardner were troopers during an epic geocache hunt and photo shoot. Thank you to Thor and Carver Emory, Casey and Brian Leonard, Graham Stoughton, Ava and Luke Tobias, and Cora Gates for participating in the Laite Beach treasure hunt photo shoot at the very last minute and especially to Casey Leonard for making all the kids smile! Thanks to Jodi, Sam, and Zoe for helping to "find gold in them thar hills" even when we were told we couldn't. The kids who attended my Treasure Hunting camp at Sweet Tree Arts: Hunter Crabtree, Miranda D'Angelo, Katie Grace Kimball, Will Laidlaw, Natalie Lindahl, Morgan Lowe, Cameron Pinchbeck, Griffin Shortall, Jack Steere, and Aidan Wyman. The Girl Scouts; Ella Tessoni, Robyn Walker-Spencer, Katherine Bowen, Lillian Dailey, Thea Allen, and Annabelle Williams, were real troopers, as always, and made amazing letter box kits.

Thank you to all my friends, family, and my wonderful community for so much support as I take on these various projects. You buy my books and say nice things and I am so grateful! Jeff, Phoebe, and Daphne, you are the buried treasure that I rediscover every day and still can't believe I really found. Eureka! ☠